DEPOSITION of
G O D

Melissa Klima

BALBOA.
PRESS

A DIVISION OF HAY HOUSE

Balboa Press books may be ordered through booksellers or by contacting:

Balboa Press
A Division of Hay House
1663 Liberty Drive
Bloomington, IN 47403
www.balboapress.com
1 (877) 407-4847

Because of the dynamic nature of the Internet, any web addresses or links contained in this transcript may have changed since publication and may no longer be valid. The views expressed in this work are solely those of the court reporter and do not necessarily reflect the views of the publisher, and the publisher hereby disclaims any responsibility for them.

This transcript is a work of non-fiction. Unless otherwise noted, the court reporter and the publisher make no explicit guarantees as to the accuracy of the information contained in this transcript and in some cases, names of people and places have been altered to protect their privacy.

The court reporter of this transcript does not dispense medical advice or prescribe the use of any technique as a form of treatment for physical, emotional, or medical problems without the advice of a physician, either directly or indirectly. The intent of the court reporter is only to offer information of a general nature to help you in your quest for emotional and spiritual well-being. In the event you use any of the information in this transcript for yourself, which is your constitutional right, the court reporter and the publisher assume no responsibility for your actions.

Any people depicted in stock imagery provided by Thinkstock are models, and such images are being used for illustrative purposes only.
Certain stock imagery © Thinkstock.

Print information available on the last page.

ISBN: 978-1-5043-8986-0 (sc)
ISBN: 978-1-5043-8988-4 (hc)
ISBN: 978-1-5043-8987-7 (e)

Library of Congress Control Number: 2017915962

Balboa Press rev. date: 11/01/2017

```
 1
 2
 3
 4
 5      -------------------------------------------------
 6
 7                      DEPOSITION OF GOD
 8                         VOLUME I
 9                      AUGUST 16, 2017
10                         6:08 AM
11
12      -------------------------------------------------
13
14
15
16
17
18
19
20
21                      MELISSA KLIMA
22                      COURT REPORTER
23
24           MINNEAPOLIS, MINNESOTA 55372
25
```

1   DISCOVERY DEPOSITION OF GOD TAKEN

2   PURSUANT TO NOTICE

3   ON AUGUST 16, 2017,

4   COMMENCING AT APPROXIMATELY 6:08 AM, BEFORE

5   MELISSA KLIMA, NOTARY PUBLIC, COUNTY OF

6   SCOTT, STATE OF MINNESOTA, TO BE USED IN THE

7   ABOVE-ENTITLED CAUSE.

8

9   A P P E A R A N C E S

10

11   MELISSA KLIMA

12   COURT REPORTER

13

14   GOD, CREATOR OF THE UNIVERSE

15

16

17

18

19

20

21

22

23

24

25

```
1              (Whereupon, the following
2              proceedings were duly had.)
3                        GOD,
4    called as a witness, having been first duly
5        sworn, deposes and says as follows:
6                    EXAMINATION
7    BY MS. KLIMA:
8    Q  Good morning. Please state your full name
9       for the record.
10   A  God, the Universe, the Divine, Elohim,
11      Supreme Being, Elah, Source, Jehovah, Lord,
12      the Almighty --
13   Q  Sorry to interrupt. You have a lot of names.
14   A  You can call me whatever name resonates with
15      you because I am all of them.
16   Q  For this deposition, are you okay with me
17      calling you "God" to keep things simple?
18   A  Yes.
19   Q  So let's dive right in. Some people think
20      that the soul enters the body when the heart
21      beats for the first time and some people
22      think it's when you take your first breath.
23      When does the soul enter the physical body?
24   A  Your soul is not housed in your physical
25      body. Your soul has always been, therefore
```

1   your physical body is housed in your soul.

2 Q Where is my soul then?

3 A Your soul is everywhere. It is not in one

4   place or the other. Your soul is

5   multidimensional. Your soul existed before

6   the creation of your physical body.

7 Q Where is my mind?

8 A Your mind is in the cells of your body. Your

9   mind is also multidimensional. There is your

10   mind, there is the matrix's mind, and there

11   is the mind of possibility. You have access

12   to them all.

13 Q Okay. So who created my body?

14 A You and I together created your body. You

15   are a miracle. Everyone is an absolute

16   beautiful miracle.

17 Q If we are absolute beautiful miracles, then

18   why do so many of us struggle with depression

19   and anxiety and feeling like we're not good

20   enough?

21 A You struggle when you forget who you really

22   are.

23 Q Why do we forget?

24 A You chose to give up your memory so you could

25   be born into the matrix of life. It is a

1   magical matrix. Just think about the ocean

2   and its vastness, dolphins, whales,

3   octopuses, sea turtles, the coral reefs, and

4   then there's the Seven Wonders of the World.

5   I could go on and on.

6 Q This world is amazing. But getting back to

7   this memory loss, so we gave up our memory so

8   we could experience this matrix of life?

9 A Yes.

10 Q So it's like a virtual reality game?

11 A Yes. There are a lot of things you cannot

12   remember, which you already know, but that is

13   exactly what makes the matrix so mysterious.

14   That is what makes it so exciting to play.

15   Life truly is one of the greatest mysteries.

16   It is one of my grandest creations.

17 Q Yeah, I'll say. It's so mysterious, it

18   scares me sometimes.

19 A Given that you do not remember where you came

20   from before you were born and you do not

21   remember where you are going after this life,

22   it makes sense that you feel scared at times,

23   but there is nothing for you to worry about.

24   You are exactly where you are supposed to be,

25   everyone is.

1   Q   Have you ever judged anyone, like felt really

2   disappointed in them?

3   A   No, I have never judged anyone and I never

4   will.

5   Q   That's a relief. A lot of people think you

6   judge them or that you're going to send them

7   to hell if they don't do what you want them

8   to do. Have you ever sent anyone to hell?

9   A   No.

10   Q   Are you ever going to send anyone to hell?

11   A   No. Actually, there is no hell. You create

12   your own hell, if you want to call it that,

13   yourself on earth with the way you think and

14   with what you choose to believe in. If you

15   choose to believe there is a hell, then there

16   is an illusion of hell for you that appears

17   real. If you choose to believe there is no

18   hell, then there is no illusion of hell for

19   you. It is all in what you decide to believe

20   in. That is part of the matrix, you get to

21   use your freewill and decide what you believe

22   in. Belief is an invisible tool that is

23   given to you when you enter the matrix.

24   Long before you were born, people

25   came up with the illusion of hell and they

1   used it to control people, and back then it

2   worked to some extent. They gained control

3   of their people by using fear, the fear of

4   hell. Hell is only an illusion. You can

5   cross hell off of your belief list.

6 Q Good, I'll gladly cross that one off. Okay,

7   so I have some questions about destiny. Is

8   there such a thing as destiny?

9 A Yes.

10 Q Can you give me an example of destiny?

11 A Yes. One example is that your kids chose you

12   before they were born. Everyone chooses

13   their parents before entering the matrix.

14 Q Can you give me another example of destiny?

15 A Yes. The body you have is destiny. You

16   chose your body before you entered the

17   matrix.

18 Q I did?

19 A Yes.

20 Q Did everyone choose their body before coming

21   into the matrix?

22 A Yes.

23 Q A lot of people seem to be upset about their

24   bodies. I hear people complaining a lot. Is

25   there more you can say about that?

1 A Everyone chose the body they have. Most of

2   you feel like it was forced upon you, like

3   somehow you got a raw deal, but everyone

4   chose it, they have just forgotten.

5 Q How can we feel better about our bodies now

6   that we are in them?

7 A By remembering that you chose it. You wanted

8   that one.

9 Q Can you tell me more about that?

10 A Think of a scuba diver. When a person goes

11   scuba diving, they have to get into their

12   gear in order to scuba dive in the ocean.

13   And before going in, they choose their gear.

14   Just like a scuba diver, you needed gear in

15   order to live in the matrix. And before

16   going in, you chose your gear.

17 Q Got it. A lot of people think that when

18   their body dies, they die with it. Do we

19   need our bodies to be alive?

20 A No.

21 Q Can you explain that further?

22 A When a scuba diver exits the water, he does

23   not die, he just does not need his gear

24   anymore. When you exit this life, you do not

25   die, you just do not need your body anymore.

```
1   Q   Wow, that actually makes sense. So was it
2       destiny that I met my husband, Jamie?
3   A   Yes, but meeting him depended on the choices
4       you made as you went along.
5   Q   You said that my kids chose me and that it
6       was destiny?
7   A   Yes. Kids choose their parents. You met
8       their dad and, at that time, your kids were
9       considering entering the matrix, and that's
10      when they chose you as their mother and him
11      as their father.
12  Q   So was I, in a sense, forced to be a parent
13      since they chose me?
14  A   No. Before you entered the matrix, you knew
15      that that is how it worked. You knew a soul
16      might choose you as their mom and you knew
17      that they might not. It is how the game is
18      set up.
19  Q   So what about sex? Don't you get pregnant
20      from having sex and then the egg gets
21      fertilized?
22  A   Yes, but there is more to it than that. If
23      no soul chose you to be their parent, at that
24      particular time, you would not be able to get
25      pregnant no matter how much sex you had.
```

```
 1   Q   Can you explain that further?

 2   A   Take a couple that has been trying to have a

 3       baby and cannot get pregnant, they knew

 4       before this life that having a baby was never

 5       a guarantee and they were fine with that.

 6       They have just forgotten now. You all have

 7       amnesia, and you are in the process of waking

 8       up. The matrix is a wild and potentially

 9       confusing game, and you all wanted to play.

10   Q   Interesting. Can you read my mind?

11   A   Absolutely, I know everything, I am God.

12       Your mind is my mind.

13   Q   My mind is your mind? That's a little over

14       my head at the moment. So is there anything

15       that surprises you?

16   A   No, nothing surprises me. I enjoy

17       experiencing life with you. There is nothing

18       you have gone through that I was not there

19       experiencing with you. I always have your

20       back. I am always in your mind even when you

21       forget I am there. I am your biggest fan.

22   Q   That's beautiful.

23       MS. KLIMA: Let's go off the record

24       for a minute.

25           (Whereupon, a recess was taken.)
```

```
1        MS. KLIMA: Okay, we're back on the
2     record.
3     BY MS. KLIMA:
4  Q  So how do you feel about having your
5     deposition taken?
6  A  I am loving the experience. You took a
7     quantum leap. You used your mind, our mind,
8     and then you jumped spiritually. Yes! More
9     and more people will start doing that. The
10    more you realize I am in your mind with you,
11    that it is actually "our" mind, the easier it
12    is to jump spiritually. How do you feel
13    about taking my deposition?
14 Q  You know, I'm supposed to be the one asking
15    questions here. But yeah, I'm feeling a
16    little nervous about this whole thing. I
17    don't like feeling nervous.
18 A  Realize feeling nervous is not a bad thing,
19    it is just one of many options of the matrix.
20 Q  Is there a way I can feel less nervous?
21 A  Yes. When you feel nervous, instantly you
22    also feel like that is a bad thing and so you
23    unconsciously add another layer of stress to
24    it. You have a beautiful complex mind. Let
25    us strip the layers down. First, strip off
```

1   the layer of thinking that feeling nervous is

2   bad, just toss that right off to the side.

3   Now that that layer is gone, just allow

4   yourself to feel nervous, do not resist it.

5   When you allow yourself to feel nervous

6   without judging it, that is when a window

7   opens up and I can come in and dissolve it

8   for you supernaturally.

9   Feelings are just feelings, they do

10   not need to be labeled good or bad. Feelings

11   are another wonderful part of the matrix of

12   life, oh so many feelings to experience.

13   Allow yourself to feel any feelings that come

14   up for you. I created feelings, there is no

15   need to be afraid of any of them. The next

16   time you feel nervous, try loving the feeling

17   and see what happens.

18 Q How do we go about loving feeling nervous?

19 A Realize that you can love it. It is possible

20   to love feeling nervous. Think bigger. If

21   you loved feeling nervous, what would happen

22   to the nervous?

23 Q It would be loved and that would change the

24   dynamic of it, and it would shift.

25 A Exactly. Everything shifts when it is loved.

1 Q   That makes sense.

2 A   The ego says, "I don't like feeling nervous,"

3   and nervous gets more nervous. The wise

4   says, "I don't mind feeling nervous," and

5   nervous relaxes. The master says, "I love

6   feeling nervous," and nervous disappears.

7 Q   That's awesome. I get it. So what's your

8   best advice for me today? And let's keep it

9   to two words. Hopefully, if it's just two

10   words, I'll remember it. I seem to have a

11   severe case of amnesia and I get distracted

12   like Dory the fish in the movie Nemo.

13 A   Have fun. The matrix is a magical place, go

14   enjoy it.

15 Q   Would that be your advice for everyone today?

16 A   Yes, have fun. When people are having fun,

17   they are peaceful. Think back to a time when

18   you were having fun, laughing, being silly.

19   Remember that time often and recreate it

20   again and again. Go have fun. While you are

21   having fun, I experience your happiness with

22   you.

23 Q   So how's my dad? Talking about having fun

24   reminded me of him.

25 A   He is happy and safe. He has his memory

1　　back. When we did his life review, he was

2　　cracking up at himself. We were both dying

3　　laughing. Get it, "dying laughing"?

4　Q　Oh my God.

5　A　Life can feel very serious while you are in

6　　it, but after it is over, it is a whole new

7　　experience. And I do have a sense of humor.

8　　I am God, I created humor. Being funny and

9　　laughing heals your worried small-me self.

10　　What? You do not think I can be funny?

11　Q　You're reading my mind. And no, not really,

12　　I've never thought of you as being funny.

13　　You're God, you're a serious person or a

14　　serious energy or a serious something, I'm

15　　not sure exactly.

16　A　Well, I have a great sense of humor. I am

17　　not worried about anything. You are the one

18　　who worries, not me. Blend with me, my

19　　child, and remember to laugh as often as you

20　　possibly can.

21　Q　I'm going to. Being too serious actually

22　　feels painful. Plus, I like this new idea of

23　　you being funny. Well, I have to go take

24　　another deposition this morning, so we'll

25　　need to take a break.

1   A   Okay, sounds good. I am ready to start back

2   up again whenever you are. I am always here

3   forever and ever.

4   Q   You're funny. Let's get to work.

5   A   Let us go, I am ready. Let us make some

6   people laugh today and show them your Godly

7   Self.

8   Q   This whole thing is a process for me, for us,

9   for whatever this matrix thing is. I still

10   have amnesia, but I'm opening up to

11   enlightenment. I wish I could just take your

12   deposition all day long, but there's bills

13   that need to be paid. Heigh-Ho, Heigh-Ho,

14   it's off to work we go. See, I can be funny

15   too.

16 A   Yes! Finally!

17   MS. KLIMA: We're off the record.

18   (Whereupon, a recess was taken.)

19   MS. KLIMA: We're back on the

20   record.

21 BY MS. KLIMA:

22 Q   So, God, I forgot to ask you this, what is

23   your date of birth?

24 A   July 15, 1970.

25 Q   That's my birthday.

1 A   I know. I was born as you that day. My

2   birthday is everybody's birthday. When

3   anyone is born, I am born. I have millions

4   of birthdays and I also have no birthday at

5   all. Does that make sense?

6 Q   No.

7 A   Within the matrix of life, I am born over and

8   over again. When a baby is born, I am born.

9   Outside of the matrix, there are no

10   birthdays. So, of course, outside of the

11   matrix, I have no birthday, nor do you. I

12   have simply always been, we have simply

13   always been. Everything about you is my DNA.

14   Everything about you is Godly energy. You

15   are me. You are me before the matrix, during

16   the matrix, and after the matrix. I am not

17   superior to you, I am you.

18 Q   I've always thought of you as superior. I

19   thought that's what you wanted. Everyone I

20   know thinks of you as superior.

21 A   If you think of me as superior, then in your

22   mind we will always be separate. You will

23   think of yourself as over there, less than

24   me, and you will think of me as over here,

25   superior to you. We cannot be as one when

1   you think like that.

2 Q   That makes sense. So how can I be you and

3   talk to you at the same time? That seems

4   crazy. I feel like that makes us separate.

5 A   It is not crazy at all, and you are not

6   separate from me. You are multidimensional,

7   I am multidimensional, we are

8   multidimensional. I was one big whole of

9   energy and I still am. I simply split off

10   some of my energy, you are that energy, and

11   because you are my energy, you are not split

12   off from me at all.

13 Q   I feel like we just went full circle.

14 A   Within the matrix, I am experiencing myself

15   in millions of different ways. It is

16   complete genius. As you look out at life,

17   you see me everywhere. I am Alpha and Omega,

18   the whole of it all. I am the small, I am

19   the large, I am everything. I am always with

20   you. I have never left you. I cannot leave

21   you when you are me.

22   MS. KLIMA: Off the record.

23   (Whereupon, a recess was taken.)

24   MS. KLIMA: Back on the record. I

25   have one more question about you being

1   everything.

2   BY MS. KLIMA:

3 Q So everyone I talk to, every person I see in

4   life is a chunk of you?

5 A Yes.

6 Q So Donald Trump is a chunk of you?

7 A That is two questions now. You said you only

8   had one more question. You would make a

9   great lawyer.

10 Q I'm being serious right now. So is Donald

11   Trump a chunk of you?

12 A Yes.

13 Q My mom is a chunk of you?

14 A Yes.

15 Q My kids are a chunk of you?

16 A Yes.

17 Q Jamie is a chunk of you?

18 A Yes.

19 Q My ex's are a chunk of you?

20 A Yes.

21 Q What about my dog, Champ, is he a small chunk

22   of you?

23 A Yes.

24 Q How can that be? And when I say "chunk," I'm

25   not being disrespectful. I'm from the farm

1   and I grew up using that word "chunk," so

2   don't be offended. Lord knows I don't want

3   God mad at me, but then again, you are me, so

4   I'm sure you're not offended because you

5   already know everything.

6 A I am definitely not offended. I am never

7   offended.

8 Q Quite frankly, this whole deposition is so

9   strange. I'm just going to get some sleep.

10   a lot of this is just too big for me at the

11   moment. Since I'm you and you're me, I guess

12   we're both going to bed; but since you're

13   everyone and everything, I guess you could be

14   staying up all night. At this moment,

15   nothing makes much sense to me, but how could

16   it? I'm just a small piece looking back at

17   its entire self. It's pretty tough to not

18   feel separate. Time for prayers before bed.

19   Thank you, God, for giving me clarity while I

20   sleep and loving me even though I feel

21   annoyed with you.

22   (Whereupon, a recess was taken.)

23   MS. KLIMA: We're back on the

24   record.

25   BY MS. KLIMA:

1 Q Good morning, God.

2 A Good morning, Beautiful.

3 Q Sorry I got annoyed with you last night.

4   It's just frustrating trying to understand

5   your testimony.

6 A That makes perfect sense that you feel

7   frustrated. Remember, I do not judge you. I

8   completely understand where you are coming

9   from. I know you have amnesia.

10 Q Of course, you do. You're me, right?

11 A Yes.

12 Q So I believe we left off with me feeling

13   separate from you and that's about the time I

14   felt really annoyed. I don't like feeling

15   separate. Sometimes I just want to come

16   home. This matrix can feel like too much

17   sometimes.

18 A Okay, let's address this separated issue.

19   You are not separate from me. Just because

20   you feel separate does not mean you are. You

21   feeling separate from me is an illusion. It

22   is not real. You cannot be separate from me

23   even if you tried. It is not possible to be

24   separate from me. You are me.

25 Q So you're saying I'm God?

1 A Yes. Whether you are big energy, small

2   energy, purple energy, green energy, I do not

3   care what label you put on my energy, it is

4   still my energy. Water is my energy, dirt is

5   my energy, trees are my energy. There is not

6   one thing you can name that is not my energy.

7   You can name and re-name and it is still all

8   mine. You can get mad at it, yell at it,

9   scream at it, and it is still all mine. You

10   can love it, hug it, kiss it, and it is still

11   all mine. You are all mine no matter what

12   you do. Does that help you understand?

13 Q Yes, actually, it does. I feel better. I

14   feel like I'm one with you. It's strange how

15   I can feel so close to you and then how I can

16   feel so separate from you at other times.

17   Can you explain why that is?

18 A Your level of awareness is increasing. You

19   are waking up, becoming more conscious. You

20   are remembering more and more who you really

21   are. You are me, you are pure love.

22 Q The more I realize I am you, the better I

23   feel.

24 A Yes. Think of the sun as being God and then

25   the rays of the sun shining out as being

1   people. The rays are still connected to the

2   sun and each ray is important. Whether the

3   ray is shining out or whether it goes back

4   into the sun, it is all still the same energy

5   and it is all still valuable. The rays are

6   never separate from the sun. You are never

7   separate from me. You are just shining out

8   into the matrix experiencing life.

9 Q I love that. Yes, that really helps me

10   understand. I'm a ray of sunshine.

11 A Yes, you are.

12 Q Still connected to you no matter what I do or

13   where I go.

14 A Exactly.

15 Q And the rays experience the sun and the sun

16   experiences the rays.

17 A Exactly, they are multidimensional. You are

18   getting it.

19 Q Everyone is a ray of sun still connected to

20   the sun?

21 A Yes, everyone, every single one.

22 Q Everything is a ray of sun still connected to

23   the sun?

24 A Yes, everything, absolutely everything.

25 Q That's beautiful, that's powerful.

1 A We are powerful.

2 Q Yes, we are. I'm going to just sit with that

3   for a while and let that soak in.

4   MS. KLIMA: Off the record.

5   (Whereupon, a recess was taken.)

6   MS. KLIMA: Back on the record.

7   BY MS. KLIMA:

8 Q It felt good to take a moment and let it sink

9   in that we are one. So I wasn't born a

10   sinner?

11 A No.

12 Q So why do people believe they were born

13   sinners? It sounds so awful when I hear

14   people say that.

15 A That is an illusion that existed before they

16   were born that was passed down to them. It

17   is a simple misunderstanding, that's all.

18   You do not like the word "sin." Just the

19   word "sin" makes you feel creepy.

20 Q Yeah, it does. I definitely don't like that

21   word.

22 A It is just a word that was used to label

23   people and things that appeared evil. The

24   majority of the people in the matrix at this

25   time live their lives under the belief system

1   of right versus wrong. They label everything

2   they view as good as "right" and they label

3   everything they view as bad as "wrong." They

4   hold on very tight to this belief system of

5   right versus wrong. Many do not know any

6   other way to live. The word "sin" means the

7   same as "wrong" to them. And the people who

8   function underneath the belief system of

9   right versus wrong, they hate to be wrong.

10 Q So they are saying that they were born a

11   sinner, meaning they were born wrong, they

12   were born bad versus good?

13 A More like they were born being capable of

14   sinning, capable of doing bad, and capable of

15   being wrong.

16 Q And isn't that true? Aren't we all capable

17   of sinning, doing bad and being wrong?

18 A In a sense, yes. Until you realize who you

19   really are, you are capable of such things.

20   All these words can be interchanged

21   and different people associate different

22   meanings with different words. So whenever

23   you talk to someone, you want to clarify what

24   definition they have put on what words.

25   People misunderstand each other all the time

1   because they assume they know what the other

2   person is thinking. Words are just words.

3   It is the meaning behind the word that

4   matters.

5   A tree is not really the word "tree,"

6   it is simply one of my beautiful creations

7   that people have labeled with the word

8   "tree." Imagine that instead of naming it

9   tree, they named it dragon. If that were the

10   case, then you would all see a tree but you

11   would say, "Oh, look at that beautiful

12   dragon." But the word "tree" was picked and

13   so now you call it that. It is not a tree or

14   a dragon, it is simply my beautiful creation.

15   Look at a tree sometime, and look beyond the

16   word you have given it, and simply experience

17   my creation as it is. No name, no label,

18   just beauty.

19 Q I like that. I'm feeling it.

20 A People love to label everything, they are not

21   sure how to function without a label, but

22   take some time to just experience people and

23   things as they are, just let them be. The

24   more you observe and experience people

25   without labeling them, the more awareness you

1 create within yourself and the more you will

2 be able to experience the true beauty of

3 life. You will see me there. You will

4 experience me in them. They will feel you

5 seeing me inside of them and it will create a

6 positive vibration between you. They will

7 have a hard time explaining in words why they

8 feel so good in your presence. They will

9 feel their own power inside of them growing.

10 You will light their fire, my fire that burns

11 within each of them. Everyone is greater

12 than they know. See their greatness, remind

13 them who they really are just with your eyes,

14 no words are needed.

15 Q What is your grandest hope for the world?

16 A That you will fully awaken, that you will

17 remember who you really are is me, pure love,

18 and you will share your remembrance with all

19 your brothers and sisters, and we will have a

20 huge celebration of life.

21 Q That sounds awesome. Using my writer and

22 taking your deposition makes me feel alive

23 and awake. Before your deposition, I was

24 told to think about what I'm good at and use

25 that for transformation. And I kept asking

1   myself, "What am I good at?"

2 A And I answered you. "You are good at court

3   reporting."

4 Q Yes, but I thought that couldn't be it

5   because court reporting is for work, not for

6   spiritual transformation.

7 A Yes, you love to argue with me.

8 Q Oh my God, I do, don't I? So it was you who

9   told me to use whatever I'm good at, work or

10   not, and use it for transformation?

11 A Yes, it was me, but remember, it was both of

12   us. You are me and I am you, we are all one.

13 Q That is so deep, but you're right. It

14   doesn't really matter if it was me or you who

15   said it because we are one in the same. I

16   was really hung up on that, I thought it had

17   to be either me or you. I kept trying to

18   keep us separate. I can be so stubborn. I

19   was like, "No, there's you and there's me."

20   But it doesn't have to be that way. There's

21   no me over here and then you over there,

22   there's just us.

23 A Exactly, you got it! The mind likes to go

24   round and round with that one.

25 Q Yeah, it does. I get it now though and the

1   less I think about it, the more I understand

2   it. Overthinking seems to block me.

3 A Overthinking is just the mind going round and

4   round, that is all. It is like the hamster

5   in the wheel. Now you are experiencing

6   oneness with me and the mind knows it. It

7   cannot really explain it, it just knows it

8   now. You "know" it beyond what words can

9   offer. Words are limited and so is the mind,

10   and it is supposed to be that way, so there

11   is nothing wrong with that. Your mind is

12   doing its job and now your higher self is

13   kicking in.

14 Q My mind feels relieved now though because it

15   knows I know, if that makes any sense.

16 A It makes sense to me.

17   MS. KLIMA: It's time for another

18   break. I'm going to enjoy feeling relieved

19   for a while.

20   GOD: And I am going to enjoy it

21   with you.

22   (Whereupon, a recess was taken.)

23   MS. KLIMA: We're back on the

24   record.

25   BY MS. KLIMA:

1   Q   So what happens when we die?

2   A   You live on. You do not need your physical

3   body to be alive.

4   Q   But what does that mean? What does that look

5   like?

6   A   I am not going to tell you that. I plead the

7   Fifth.

8   Q   Why won't you tell me?

9   A   If you rented a movie, would you ever watch

10   it from the ending to the beginning?

11   Q   No.

12   A   Why not?

13   Q   Because it would ruin the whole movie. I

14   would know what was going to happen.

15   A   Exactly. The same applies to your life. You

16   do not get to know the ending, it is not time

17   to know yet. That would take all the fun out

18   of the experience of life for you.

19   Q   True. If I knew the ending, it would take

20   all the suspense out of it.

21   A   And not knowing the ending of the movie is

22   not scary, it is exciting. And like that,

23   not knowing the ending of your life is not

24   scary, it is exciting. Not knowing is one of

25   the coolest parts.

1 Q So life is like a movie?

2 A That is one way of looking at it.

3 Q I thought you said it was a matrix?

4 A Yes, that is another way of understanding it.

5 Q So which is it?

6 A It is both. You really are stuck in a habit
7   of making things one way or the other. There
8   are multiple ways of looking at life. Words
9   are just words. It is the experience that
10   matters. You are experiencing life, creating
11   as you go, and you will know as you go.

12 Q I don't create everything though. Some
13   things just happen that I have no control
14   over.

15 A Yes, that is true in a sense, but you are
16   connected to everything. You do have options
17   regarding how you react to those things that
18   happen and how you react matters because your
19   reaction influences what happens next. It is
20   to your advantage to react positively to
21   everything.

22 Q But how can anyone like when bad things
23   happen?

24 A They do not necessarily like it at first, but
25   the wise make the best of it. They find the

1   good in everything and they benefit greatly

2   for doing that.

3 Q This is off the track here, but are there

4   ghosts? I saw a ghost when I was little. It

5   floated across my room and went right through

6   the door.

7 A Why do you ask me if there are ghosts when

8   you saw one for yourself?

9 Q Good point. Some of my friends have seen

10   them too. So what are they? I know we've

11   labeled them "ghosts," but what are they?

12 A Everything is me. They are my energy. They

13   are a part of the matrix, the movie that you

14   are starring in.

15 Q Can we predict the future?

16 A Yes, to some degree.

17 Q How?

18 A Spend time visioning what you want in the

19   future as if it has already happened. Use

20   your imagination again. I know as a kid you

21   were told to stop pretending, to grow up,

22   that things were just your imagination. They

23   talked as if your imagination was silly and

24   useless, but it is powerful and I highly

25   recommend you start using your imagination

1   again. Also, take time to write down on a

2   piece of paper how you want things to be in a

3   year from now or five years from now or even

4   a week from now. Write it out as if it has

5   already happened the way you want it to.

6 Q I did that before I met Jamie. I wrote down

7   what I wanted in a man and within that year

8   of writing it, he came into my life, so I do

9   have experience that it works.

10 A I know you do, I just wanted to jog your

11   memory. It really does work.

12   MS. KLIMA: I'm going to go

13   meditate for a while and I have some other

14   things I need to go do.

15   GOD: I am going with you. It is

16   impossible for you to go anywhere without me.

17   (Whereupon, a recess was taken.)

18   MS. KLIMA: Back on the record.

19 BY MS. KLIMA:

20 Q Why is it again that I don't feel like I'm

21   good enough sometimes?

22 A Because you forget who you really are. Did

23   you forget again?

24 Q Yes. Please explain again.

25 A When you entered the matrix, you gave up your

```
1      memory of where you came from and who you
2      really are. You did that on purpose, you
3      chose to do that.
4  Q   Why?
5  A   Because you wanted to experience the matrix,
6      you wanted to experience life. In order to
7      play, you have to give up your memory.
8  Q   And what's the point of that again?
9  A   Because it creates the opportunity for you to
10     experience "not knowing" and to then
11     experience "remembering."
12 Q   Why would I want to experience "not knowing"?
13 A   Because you knew everything and you wanted to
14     experience something different.
15 Q   That does kind of make sense.
16 A   Before you were born, you knew everything.
17     You knew you were me and you knew how awesome
18     you are. Now you have the opportunity to
19     choose me instead of just being me.
20 Q   So if I'm understanding you, it's like I'm a
21     small version of you experiencing myself as
22     small with the opportunity to experience
23     myself as big, as the whole you, which is
24     actually me?
25 A   Yes.
```

1 Q   It seems complicated.

2 A   It is but it is not. It can be both. It

3   does not have to be one way or the other. It

4   just is the way it is.

5 Q   It is the way it is?

6 A   Yes, accept the matrix as it is.

7 Q   Got it. What's the most insane thing I've

8   ever done?

9 A   Argue with what already is. That is pure

10   insanity at its finest, but it is easy to

11   slip into insanity when you are operating as

12   your small-me self. When you blend your

13   small-me self with your big-me self, you

14   become your big-me self fully and then you

15   remember who you really are. It is like

16   turning on the lights in a dark room. "Aha"

17   you can see.

18 Q   Got it. And by "big-me self," you are

19   referring to what some people call their

20   highest self or higher power or source?

21 A   Yes, you can use whatever word you want to

22   try and explain it. Small/big.

23   Lower/higher. Person/God. You/me.

24   Subconscious/conscious. You can get all

25   tangled up with words or you can just keep it

1 simple. You are good enough. You have

2 always been good enough. Of course, you are

3 good enough, you are me, you are my DNA. You

4 are awesome. You always will be awesome, you

5 cannot not be. Thinking you are not good

6 enough is an illusion. Do you remember how

7 your mom would hang the clothes to dry on the

8 clothes line in the summer?

9 Q Yes, I loved walking through the sheets

10 letting them float across my face smelling

11 the freshness of clean sheets.

12 A That is another way to dissolve feeling not

13 good enough, just walk through it like it is

14 a sheet hanging on the clothes line. It is

15 not solid, it is an illusion. All fear is an

16 illusion.

17 Q Got it. Okay, so how about the past, should

18 I worry about the past or feel bad about

19 things I've done in the past that I'm not so

20 proud of?

21 A No.

22 Q Not even a little bit?

23 A Not even a little bit.

24 Q Why?

25 A Beating yourself up for something you have

1   done in the past is not good use of our

2   energy. That is not blending with me, that

3   is pulling away, that is curling up into your

4   small-me self, and that is why you do not

5   feel good when you start beating yourself up.

6   It is an option you can use while playing in

7   the matrix, but it is not an option you have

8   to choose. People choose it all the time,

9   but I do not recommend it.

10 Q Don't I learn something from the past by

11   recognizing that I was bad, then beating

12   myself up for it, and then starting new

13   again?

14 A That is one way to do it, but you do not stop

15   beating yourself up, you keep being mad at

16   yourself over and over and over again. This

17   is definitely not the most effective way.

18 Q So what's a better more effective way?

19 A Realize the past is complete, it is over.

20   You cannot go back and change the past.

21   Really let that sink in. I will say it again

22   to help it sink into your psyche. The past

23   is complete, the past is over. And one more

24   time for clarity purposes, the past is

25   complete, the past is over. The past will

1   never happen again like that, never again

2   just like that ever again.

3 Q It does feel good to really realize it's over

4   and complete. I am feeling very present.

5 A Excellent. Remember, you did the best you

6   could back then. All you knew was what you

7   knew then and you used what you knew to do

8   what you did. You could not have done it any

9   other way back then. Give yourself a break.

10 Cut yourself some slack. That is an order

11 from me, God. If you want to honor me, then

12 honor yourself because we are one. You were

13 operating as the small-me back then, you were

14 not fully aware of the whole. It is not your

15 fault. You did the best you could.

16   Every person is always doing the best

17 they can at any given moment with what their

18 level of awareness is. There are no

19 exceptions to this rule. There are no

20 monsters, there are no mistakes, there are no

21 villains. There are only different levels of

22 awareness. When you get that, when you

23 really get that, you forgive yourself and you

24 forgive everyone. Only then do the shackles

25 of the past drop to the floor and only then

1   can you start anew.

2   If you want to help people, do not

3   judge them, do not call them names. Whenever

4   you curse someone, you curse me, you curse

5   yourself. We are all one. Think bigger. If

6   you want to master the matrix, you need to

7   think big, think really big.

8 Q So when someone does something bad or mean, I

9   should instantly forgive them?

10 A Yes.

11 Q I don't know if I can do that. My judgy self

12   comes rushing in pretty darn fast. It comes

13   so fast that sometimes I'm not even aware of

14   it until after some time has passed.

15 A I have faith in you. You will eventually

16   master it. Recognize it is all about their

17   level of awareness at that moment, and your

18   ability to forgive is all about your level of

19   awareness.

20 Q What about murderers, we should forgive them?

21 A Yes. Put them in jail and focus on reforming

22   them, focus on helping them wake up.

23 Q So it was their level of awareness or lack

24   thereof that caused them to do it?

25 A Yes. Instead of judging people and calling

1   them names, switch your attention to helping

2   increase people's level of awareness. Do you

3   want to help or do you want to be part of the

4   dilemma?

5 Q I want to help.

6 A Excellent. You have no idea what they went

7   through as a child, what they went through as

8   an adult, you have no clue, but the whole of

9   me does. They are still my children.

10   Everyone is my creation no matter how well

11   you think they are doing within the matrix of

12   life. What you do not understand is that you

13   are part of the dilemma.

14 Q I'm part of the dilemma?

15 A Yes, your level of awareness affects other

16   people's level of awareness. The more aware

17   you become, the more aware the world becomes,

18   and so it is with everyone's level of

19   awareness. You all impact each other.

20 Q Can you explain more about how we all impact

21   each other?

22 A Within the matrix, the Law of the Domino

23   Effect applies. What you do affects another.

24   Just like when you toss a pebble into the

25   water and it ripples outward, so it is with

1   you. You matter. Everyone matters.

2   Everyone in the matrix is on the same team,

3   they just have not realized that yet; and

4   therefore, they treat their teammates

5   horribly at times. Murderers are not just

6   murderers, they are your teammates. The

7   matrix is a team. Think bigger.

8 Q If you could define a murderer in one word,

9   what word would that be?

10 A Unconscious. They are suffering at a level

11   that you cannot even imagine. At the end of

12   their time in the matrix, I will do a life

13   review with them myself, personally. At that

14   time, their small-me self will be blended

15   with their big-me self and they will get

16   their memory back. They will say, "I was

17   blind, but now I see." But how great would

18   it feel to see, to really see before you exit

19   the matrix?

20 Q It would be awesome. I want to see, to see

21   bigger than I can even imagine. I'm excited

22   to go out in the world today and create,

23   create and experience life.

24 A Excellent! And remember, I am in your mind,

25   I am in your heart, I am in every step you

1   take, every breath you take. I am literally

2   you.

3 Q I'm getting my memory back. What's your best

4   advice for today?

5 A Go find a homeless person on the street and

6   see me in him, see yourself in him. Ask him

7   what happened that led him to being on the

8   street, and let me know later how it all

9   goes.

10 Q You're already going to know though because

11   you're right there with me.

12 A That is true, but it is not just about you

13   and I knowing. It is about the whole world

14   knowing.

15 Q What is that supposed to mean now?

16 A You know what I mean.

17 Q I know I do, but I don't want to admit it.

18 A Why?

19 Q Because it scares me. It scares the small

20   me.

21 A I know, but it also excites you.

22 Q Yes, sometimes. Thinking about your

23   deposition being made a public record scares

24   me by 80 percent and excites me by 20

25   percent.

1　A　You will be fine. It is not time yet anyway

2　　　so do not worry about it.

3　Q　I have more blending to do with you. I can't

4　　　even think about anyone reading your

5　　　transcript because then I feel like stopping

6　　　this whole deposition. You're entitled to

7　　　your privacy and maybe you should think about

8　　　exercising that right.

9　A　So now the small me is advising the big me on

10　　what to do?

11　Q　Yes, I guess so. This is crazy, this whole

12　　Q&A between us is kind of crazy, isn't it?

13　A　No, it is not. Everybody does it. Some of

14　　them are just not as aware of it as you are.

15　Q　Exactly.

16　A　But there are others who are very aware, and

17　　they took the spiritual leap and are

18　　expressing their awareness publically in

19　　their own unique way. They are using their

20　　gifts and sharing their gifts.

21　Q　So why do I have to do it then?

22　A　Because it is what you came here to do. It

23　　is your destiny. You are gifted. Everyone

24　　is gifted. You are a court reporter, you

25　　take down testimony, and you transcribe it.

1   You are the keeper of the record.

2 Q But people who haven't realized that they are

3   you are going to read what you just testified

4   to and not understand it. The portion of you

5   that's currently operating as a smaller

6   version of you is not going to understand

7   you. Then all the small you's are going to

8   potentially judge me.

9 A Everyone will be fine. Deep down they all

10   know who they really are. It is time to

11   start stirring up the deep-down part of them.

12 Q I was taught to not stir the pot.

13 A You were taught to not stir the pot in a

14   negative way. Making this transcript a

15   public record is stirring the pot in a Godly

16   high-vibrational spiritual way. When it is

17   time, you will be ready.

18 Q Okay, I'll take your word for it. I'm just

19   going to have faith. You are God after all.

20 A Yes, please do. Trust in me and the best

21   life will unfold right before your eyes, just

22   like magic.

23   MS. KLIMA: And we're off the

24   record.

25   GOD: And we are off to experience

1   life.

2   (Whereupon, a recess was taken.)

3   MS. KLIMA: And we're back from

4   experiencing life and we're back on the

5   record.

6   BY MS. KLIMA:

7   Q One thing I've realized is we're always

8   putting meaning on everything. If someone

9   does something, right away we're deciding

10   what that means. Can you explain what

11   meaning is all about?

12 A Yes, it is part of the matrix. It can be

13   used for entertainment or you can use it to

14   torture yourself or anything else in between.

15   You use your freewill to decide what

16   everything means. There are a lot of options

17   when deciding what something means. One

18   thing can mean something completely different

19   to another person. Nothing actually has any

20   meaning except the meaning you put on it.

21 Q So the meaning I put on something isn't even

22   true?

23 A No, it is not. It is true for you at that

24   very moment only because you say so, but it

25   is not the truth overall. It is an option

1   that you chose, so you believe it to be true,

2   but it is not rock-solid true. Think of it

3   like this, there are at least five different

4   ways to look at anything that happens. Let

5   us call it the "Freewill Five." Hopefully

6   giving it a name will help you remember.

7   When you experience life through the

8   Freewill Five, you can experience what

9   freewill really is. Freewill is the freedom

10   to choose. You do not have the freedom to

11   choose when you think there is only one way.

12   When you realize there are at least five

13   different ways to look at something, you

14   experience freedom of choice within your own

15   mind and that is powerful. You become

16   unstuck. You clear the block.

17   A wise person, a person with expanded

18   awareness, knows this and enjoys a life of

19   freedom within and freedom without. When

20   they come across a person who is opinionated,

21   they are not bothered by that person. They

22   never argue with anyone. They realize that

23   person is experiencing life with limited

24   awareness. They realize that person has no

25   idea what the Freewill Five even is, and so

```
1    they have compassion for that person.
2       So if you want to experience wisdom
3    and experience freedom, then never argue with
4    a person, simply realize they are not aware
5    that there are at least five ways to look at
6    something. They are stuck thinking there is
7    only one way, they are stuck thinking that
8    their way is the only way. We know their way
9    is not the only way, but they do not. They
10   do not know what they do not know and it is
11   not their fault, they are just sleeping. Be
12   gentle with those who sleep. Be aware of
13   those who sleep.
14 Q Got it. That makes sense. So is it possible
15   to not put a meaning on something, to let it
16   mean nothing at all?
17 A Yes.
18 Q How do I do that? How do I make something
19   meaningless?
20 A When it dawns on you that there are at least
21   five ways to look at everything, in that
22   moment, you are floating between the five.
23   You are floating in the Freewill Five. Float
24   around and look at your options. You can see
25   them all, but you choose none. In that
```

1   moment of observing all five ways to react,

2   you are not reacting at all and you are

3   experiencing the nothingness of it. It is a

4   beautiful space to be in. You are

5   experiencing enlightenment in that moment.

6   You are being nothing. It feels light and

7   right to just be.

8   In that moment of awareness, in that

9   moment of just being, you can then choose to

10   roll back into creating, roll back into

11   creating by choosing one of the five options

12   that works best for you. The wise one

13   chooses the option that makes them feel the

14   best. They choose the option that is for

15   their highest good and for the highest good

16   of everyone.

17 Q That makes sense to me. That's empowering.

18   You said at least five, so there's more than

19   five ways to look at every situation?

20 A Oh, yes, way more than five, but I said five

21   so your mind can grasp it, so you can

22   understand it.

23 Q I like the space of not choosing any option,

24   it feels light. It feels quiet and still. I

25   feel so present.

1 A The present is a "present."

2 Q Yes, it really is.

3 A Your awareness is increasing. We experience

4   our oneness when we float around our options

5   choosing none.

6 Q Wow, that's really powerful. Can you lay it

7   out in a simple step-by-step process?

8 A Step one, realize there are always at least

9   five ways to look at a situation. Step two,

10   enjoy knowing that you have options. Step

11   three, create a healthy way to look at it.

12   Step four, take positive action. Step five,

13   love your life. Live your life using the

14   Freewill Five. It is your invisible tool.

15   It is a very powerful tool. It saves

16   relationships, it saves lives. Remember, you

17   are all on the same team. Go, Team Matrix!

18 Q Got it. So growing up, I remember hearing in

19   church about judgment day. Judgment day is

20   coming or something to that effect. What is

21   that all about? Is there a judgment day for

22   all mankind?

23 A There is not a judgment day like you are

24   thinking of it in that context. You thought

25   it meant that there was one day that I would

1   come down and judge all of you, and that is

2   not going to happen. I do not judge anyone.

3   Q   So when it talks about judgment day in the

4   bible, what is that referring to?

5   A   That is fear based and people said there was

6   a judgment day to scare people into doing and

7   behaving the way they wanted them to. You

8   can relax, there is no judgment day. I am

9   not going to fly down from the sky and be mad

10   at everyone, and I am not going to send

11   anyone to a burning pit of fire. I did not

12   create my very own creation to then get mad

13   at my very own creation. I know exactly what

14   I am doing.

15 Q   Okay, good. Thank you for clearing that up.

16   So you testified that you are everything.

17   What about my dog? Are you my dog too?

18 A   You already asked that, and yes, I am.

19 Q   Are you a spider?

20 A   Yes.

21 Q   Are you a truck driving by?

22 A   Yes.

23 Q   Are you the rain?

24 A   Yes.

25 Q   The snow?

```
1   A   Yes.

2   Q   Are you sadness?

3   A   Yes.

4   Q   Are you anxiety?

5   A   Yes.

6   Q   Are you happiness?

7   A   Yes.

8   Q   Are you cancer?

9   A   Yes.

10  Q   I thought God was only the good. If you're

11      cancer, that seems bad. So you're saying you

12      are good and bad?

13  A   Yes, I am saying that I am everything. Do

14      you think I am only the God of the good?

15  Q   Yes, I guess so.

16  A   If you believe in two Creators, the God of

17      the good and some other God of the bad, that

18      creates duality in your mind and you feel

19      conflict within. There are not two Creators

20      of the Universe. There is only me. There is

21      nothing that I am not. I am everything that

22      is, everything that was, and I am everything

23      that ever will be. I am the matrix itself, I

24      am everything in it, and I am everything

25      outside of it. I am the field of
```

possibility. There is only one God and I am
it. I am greater than your mind can imagine.
I am greater than any definition you can come
up with. I am greater than any concept. I
am so awesome that I am unexplainable.

Q So should I just give up trying to figure you
out then?

A Sure, if that makes you feel better.

Q Well, I don't want to. I like trying to
figure you out.

A I know. It is your passion.

Q It is my passion, and I don't want to give it
up.

A Then do not.

Q I'm feeling annoyed with you again.

A I know. You will be fine. Your awareness
expands and contracts. You are exactly where
you are supposed to be.

Q I'm not sure what to ask you right now. I'm
perplexed just sitting here thinking. Why
would you create a matrix with cancer in it?

A The matrix is the matrix. It is what it is.
You wanted to experience the matrix. You
were fully aware of what could happen. You
knew cancer was a possibility and you still

```
1        wanted to play. You are acting like a victim
2        now, like somehow I forced you into it. You
3        were never forced to play, you wanted to.
4        You are not a victim of anything.
5   Q    Why don't I remember that?
6   A    Like I said before, you gave up your memory
7        on purpose. You cannot enter the matrix
8        with your memory, it would ruin the game. If
9        you had your memory, it would be impossible
10       to begin playing the game.
11  Q    Oh, that's right. I keep forgetting that
12       part. Is this a good time to remember the
13       Freewill Five?
14  A    Yes, please do. You were given freewill so
15       you could always transcend any situation that
16       you perceive as negative.
17  Q    Step one, realize I have options. Okay, I'm
18       remembering that I have options.
19  A    Yes.
20  Q    Step two, enjoy knowing that I have options
21       and that I don't have to pick any. I'm
22       floating around. I'm enjoying this freedom
23       of no choice. I'm feeling better. I'm
24       flying around like a bird. I think I just
25       want to stay here in step two. It feels good
```

1   to just "be." There's no resistance. It's

2   just peaceful. So how long can I just "be"?

3 A As long as you want.

4 Q As long as I want?

5 A Yep.

6 Q You're not supposed to say "yep" in a

7   deposition. It's supposed to be "yes" or

8   "no." It can be confusing later when you

9   read your transcript otherwise.

10 A Well, thank you for that. Glad to see you

11   are getting your sense of humor back.

12 Q Now step three, create an empowering way to

13   look at the situation. So I was looking at

14   me trying to figure you out as annoying, you

15   actually being annoying and me feeling

16   annoyed by your annoyingness. That's one of

17   the five options, and I didn't feel good with

18   that option.

19 A And you never will feel good when you look at

20   me or anyone else as being annoying.

21 Q True. So another way to look at it is that

22   you're not annoying at all. You are a

23   beautiful mystery and I know that it's okay

24   if I don't know everything.

25 A Yes, and that is knowing. You know that you

1   do not always know, and that is knowing

2   something.

3 Q That's deep. Good point. Yes, I like that.

4   I'm feeling light and right. Okay, and then

5   there's step four, take positive action. I

6   will keep meditating, keep writing, keep

7   seeing God in everyone, and love not knowing,

8   love the mystery.

9 A Excellent! And remember, you will continue

10   to awaken. There is more coming. There is

11   always more coming, but be thankful for the

12   amount of awareness that you do have right

13   now. You are aware that you are aware.

14 Q That's exciting. And step five, love your

15   life, enjoy your life. Perfect. Wow, the

16   Freewill Five really does work. It's like

17   you're stuck in a ditch and then the Freewill

18   Five tow truck shows up and pulls you out,

19   and then you're back on the road cruising

20   down the highway with your hair blowing in

21   the wind.

22 A You got it. Your awareness keeps growing.

23 Q So we haven't really talked about this, but I

24   am starting to be able to see the air.

25   Before, it was like there was nothing between

1   me and say, for example, the table, but now,

2   I am aware of the space, the air between me

3   and the table. It's like it's alive or

4   something. It moves, kind of shakes, like

5   vibrates. It's hard to explain. What's up

6   with that?

7 A You are becoming aware of energy itself.

8   Keep observing it without judgement. It is

9   all good, there is nothing for you to worry

10   about.

11   MS. KLIMA: Okay, off the record

12   again.

13   (Whereupon, a recess was taken.)

14   MS. KLIMA: Back on the record.

15   BY MS. KLIMA:

16 Q Have I ever played the matrix before? People

17   talk about reincarnation. Have I ever been

18   in the matrix before?

19 A Yes, you have.

20 Q Why don't I remember being here before?

21 A If I had an attorney representing me, she

22   would object as being asked and answered.

23   You gave up your memory when you entered the

24   matrix, remember?

25 Q Oh, that's right. I remember now. I

1   remember that I don't remember doing that.

2 A Excellent, you are aware that you are aware

3   that you gave up your memory in order to

4   play.

5 Q Have other people been in the matrix before?

6 A Yes.

7 Q Some people do past-life readings, so do they

8   remember?

9 A No one fully remembers at this point, but

10   everyone is starting to remember more and

11   more.

12 Q I don't remember my past lives. Why can't

13   you just let me remember everything?

14 A If you remembered everything, would it be

15   possible for you to experience having faith?

16 Q I guess not, no, because then I'd know

17   everything.

18 A Exactly. Before this life, you wanted to

19   experience having faith.

20 Q What does it mean to have faith?

21 A It means you somehow magically just know that

22   everything is going to be all right. Even

23   though you do not have all the answers and

24   even though sometimes the situation may look

25   gloomy, you still have faith that everything

1   is okay and will be okay. Somehow, someway
2   everything will be okay. In a lawsuit,
3   attorneys need evidence to believe something.
4   Faith is believing with no evidence.
5 Q Why couldn't I have just experienced faith
6   before I got here?
7 A Because you knew everything before you got
8   here.
9 Q Oh yeah, that's right. Good grief, it's so
10   simple after all.
11 A Yes, it is. Faith can only be experienced
12   when you do not remember.
13 Q Okay, so this next question is a big one.
14   Have you ever judged someone who has had an
15   abortion?
16 A No. I know exactly what led them to make
17   that decision. I know everything. My love
18   is unconditional, that means I love you all
19   no matter what you have done.
20 Q Is it ever helpful to judge someone?
21 A No. If you judge anyone, including yourself,
22   you experience a feeling of disgust and
23   regret, and then poison is released into your
24   bloodstream and it literally hurts your
25   physical body. It is a law of the matrix.

1   Q   Is that what it's referring to in the bible

2   when it talks about how in the same way you

3   judge others, you will be judged?

4   A   Yes. Judging anyone has its very own

5   consequences and they are not to your

6   advantage. And it is true that holding a

7   grudge against someone releases poison into

8   your physical body. Being mad or upset with

9   someone actually hurts you.

10   Q   Okay, got it. We're going to switch gears

11   here. So what's the best way to handle the

12   problems we have in our lives?

13   A   Stop calling them problems. When things do

14   not go the way you want them to, right away

15   you call it a problem. The truth is that

16   every problem, as you call it, is actually an

17   opportunity.

18   Q   That sounds fluffy. I've had plenty of

19   problems. So you're saying I've never had

20   problems?

21   A   You have never had problems, only

22   opportunities. You keep yourself locked into

23   problems, as you call them, by calling them

24   "problems." You do it to yourself without

25   even realizing it. Everything is an

1   opportunity, know this and you shall

2   experience salvation.

3 Q I have heard people say that before, I just

4   didn't really believe them.

5 A Well, believe them. It was me talking to you

6   when they said that. I talk to you through

7   other people too. The truth is that there

8   are no problems, only opportunities. What

9   would the world be like if you knew that

10   everything was an opportunity?

11 Q It would be awesome.

12 A Well, now you know. Think big. Think like

13   the God you are.

14   MS. KLIMA: We have to go off the

15   record again. Lots of stuff going on in the

16   matrix. Lots of opportunities, I mean. And

17   we're off.

18   (Whereupon, a recess was taken.)

19   BY MS. KLIMA:

20 Q So on to my next question, how do you feel

21   about money? Is money good or bad?

22 A It is neither. It just is. It is part of

23   the matrix, period. It gets you things you

24   need to survive, like food and water, and it

25   gets you stuff you think you want. Whatever

material things you buy with money, you
cannot take any of it with you once you exit
the matrix, so enjoy material things, but do
not get attached because they must stay
within the matrix.

Think of money with the Freewill Five
options, five options floating in the air
above your head. Create five different
beliefs about money and then choose the
belief that best serves you, that best serves
you and your teammates.

One of the most powerful tools you
have is your ability to believe. Whatever
you believe in, the matrix will copy you.
You choose what you believe in and then
manifestation begins. Create a belief and
the matrix will echo it back to you. If you
believe you are not good enough, then you are
not. If you believe money is evil, then you
surely will not have any. If you keep
telling yourself you have money problems,
then you will keep having money problems. If
you believe there is no such thing as a good
man, then you will not have one. The matrix
copies you. It is the law of the matrix and

1   it cannot be changed. You received the

2   golden ticket of freewill when you were born.

3   The most successful people are using their

4   golden ticket.

5   Q So what do people do who really are having

6   financial problems at this moment? The

7   matrix keeps copying their situation, so how

8   do they get out of that copying cycle of

9   financial problems?

10   A The Freewill Five. Remember, there are

11   always at least five ways to look at a

12   situation. They are choosing one way. There

13   are at least four other ways to look at their

14   financial situation. Step one, realize there

15   are other ways to look at it. Step two,

16   float about for a while enjoying not having

17   an opinion about it. Step three, create an

18   empowering way to look at it. For example,

19   say to yourself, "You know what? I do have

20   enough money right now. You know why I know

21   that? Because I am alive and that is proof

22   that I have had enough because I am still

23   here." Now the universe just copied that

24   thought and supernaturally doubled it. Now

25   you have shifted from believing you do not

1   have enough to realizing that you do, in

2   fact, have enough. Now say to yourself,

3   "Thank you, God, for getting me this far."

4   Now the universe just copied that thought and

5   supernaturally doubled it. You have shifted

6   into gratitude. Now say to yourself, "Thank

7   you, God, for the money that is coming to me

8   very soon." Now the universe just copied

9   that thought and supernaturally doubled it.

10 You have shifted again. Now you have faith.

11 Step four, take positive action, which you

12 already have by praying with faith that money

13 is coming to you very soon and being grateful

14 for whatever amount you do have, but there is

15 more you can do. Now go out into the matrix

16 and find someone who has less money than you.

17 There are people out there with less money

18 than you. Go find them and give them some of

19 yours. I do not care how much you give them,

20 but give them something. Once you do that,

21 you shift again from being the

22 I-do-not-have-enough person to being the one

23 who has enough. The universe copies that and

24 supernaturally doubles it. Step five, love

25 your life just as it is and then a door

1   opens. Live your life using the Freewill

2   Five. It is your invisible tool, a very

3   powerful tool.

4 Q I get that. It makes sense.

5   MS. KLIMA: I'm going to make an

6   outline of the Freewill Five and have it

7   marked as an exhibit.

8   (Whereupon, God Deposition

9   Exhibit No. 1 was marked for

10   identification.)

11   BY MS. KLIMA:

12 Q I have one last question.

13 A I have heard that before.

14 Q So is there for real without a doubt a life

15   after this one?

16 A Absolutely.

17 Q Wait, I do have more questions.

18 A I knew it.

19 Q So how can I know that? I know I can have

20   faith and just know it to be true without

21   proof, but is there anything else you can say

22   about forever? Forever is a hard concept to

23   understand because everything here has

24   endings.

25 A Yes. Imagine you are going up into space and

```
1        as you are flying up into space, you come to
2        a wall. What is behind the wall?
3    Q   More space. There has to be something behind
4        the wall.
5    A   Exactly. So imagine yourself moving through
6        the wall and you keep flying up higher into
7        space and then you come to another wall.
8        What is behind that wall?
9    Q   More space.
10   A   Exactly. And, once again, you move through
11       the wall and you keep flying up even higher
12       and you come to another wall. What is behind
13       that wall?
14   Q   More space.
15   A   Exactly. And, once again, you move through
16       the wall and you keep flying up even higher
17       and you come to another wall. What is behind
18       that wall?
19   Q   More space.
20   A   Exactly. And, once again, you move through
21       that wall and you keep flying up --
22   Q   Wow! I get it. There's always going to be
23       something.
24   A   Exactly. It cannot end. There is no end.
25       You just experienced forever.
```

1   Q   Okay, one last question and I mean it this
2   time. Am I the only one who can take your
3   deposition?
4   A   Absolutely not. I will speak to anyone who
5   has questions. I speak to everyone, they
6   just have not realized it yet, but they will.
7   MS. KLIMA: I have no further
8   questions at this time, but I would like to
9   leave the record open in case some questions
10   come up in the future.
11   GOD: Sounds good. I am always
12   available, forever and ever.
13   MS. KLIMA: I would like to end
14   with a prayer. Thank you, God, for the
15   clarity and guidance that is coming to me
16   now. Thank you, God, for the clarity and
17   guidance that is coming to every person who
18   reads your deposition transcript. Thank you,
19   God, for allowing us to realize that we are
20   truly one with you, one with each other, and
21   one with everything. Go, Team Matrix! Amen.
22   GOD: The matrix just copied you
23   and supernaturally doubled it. Amen.
24   (Whereupon, the proceedings were
25   ended.)

1   STATE OF MINNESOTA)

2   )

3   COUNTY OF SCOTT   )

4   REPORTER'S CERTIFICATE

5

6   I, MELISSA KLIMA, do hereby certify that

7   the above and foregoing transcript, consisting of

8   the preceding 66 pages is a correct transcript of

9   my stenograph notes, and is a full, true, and

10   complete transcript of the proceedings to the best

11   of my ability.

12

13

14

15

16   WITNESS MY HAND AND SEAL this _____

17   day of _____, 20 _____.

18

19

20   _____

21   MELISSA KLIMA

22   Notary Public, Scott County, Minnesota

23   My Commission Expires January 31, 2020

24

25

THE FREEWILL FIVE

The Freewill Five is a five-step path to enlightenment. You can use the Freewill Five to improve any situation in your life that is making you feel negative. Here's how to do it:

STEP ONE:

This is hugely important. Remember that there are at least five different ways to look at a situation or person and remember that right now you are choosing one.

List below the current way you are looking at the situation or person that is stressing you out.

1. _____

_____

_____

_____

_____

_____

STEP TWO:

List below four other ways you could look at that situation or person if you were to think positive uplifting thoughts. I know it's tough to think positive when you feel negative, but you can do it. I have faith in you.

2. _____

_____

_____

_____

_____

_____

3. _____

_____

_____

_____

_____

_____

4. _____

_____

_____

_____

_____

5. _____

_____

_____

_____

_____

Now that you remember that there are at least five different ways to look at this situation or person, I want you to choose none of them, do not choose any. Just float around the five different ways, knowing they are there but do not choose any. Take a break and have no opinion. Allow yourself to enjoy this space of freedom, this beautiful space of not choosing. There is a wonderful sense of freedom when you choose to not choose. Take all the time you want to enjoy this space of nothingness. It may feel uncomfortable at first to not choose, but allow yourself to float around between all your options. This is where your true freedom is.

STEP THREE:

When you are ready, roll back into creating and list below the way to view the situation or person that serves you best, that makes you feel happy and uplifted. Being positive is to your advantage. I have faith in you.

_____

_____

_____

_____

_____

_____

STEP FOUR:

Take positive action. What can you do next to stay positive? List below some positive actions you can take that will continue to benefit you and keep you feeling good about this situation or person. I have faith in you.

_____

_____

_____

_____

_____

_____

STEP FIVE:

Enjoy your life. Joy is your sacred right, choose it. I have faith in you.

~ Melissa Klima

Visit me at www.depositionofgod.com

About The Court Reporter

As a professional court reporter, Melissa Klima takes her job as the "keeper of the record" very seriously. She began her court reporting career in 1990 in the Alexandria, Minnesota area. After reporting for a number of years, Melissa moved to Minneapolis and founded Chaser Court Reporting, Inc., in 1998.

Born and raised on a farm in Hancock, Minnesota, Melissa loved to ride horse and play with her dogs. In high school, she played basketball and ran track. Melissa's background was Lutheran and going to church was a big part of her family life growing up. As an adult, what became important to her was not the name that was placed on a certain religion, but the deep connection she felt with God.

Currently residing in Prior Lake, Minnesota with her husband and their four children, Melissa continues to be an active court reporter and is currently taking the Deposition of God, Volume II.

www.depositionofgod.com

Printed in the United States
By Bookmasters